THESIS WRITING: HOW TO WRITE AN EXCELLENT THESIS

WORK – LIFE BALANCE: A LOOK AT TEACHERS' SPILLOVER EFFECTS

BY FREALYN M. NAVARRO

I0417624

The authors of this book aim to help the graduating students in thesis writing guide with the example of own submitted work when they were studying Master in Educational Management.

TABLE OF CONTENTS

PART I. OVERVIEW OF THESIS WRITING

Thesis writing is one of the most challenging parts of graduating students' life. This is something that a student has to focus his/her efforts in getting the necessary information in relation to the topic he/she selected to research on. Tough, is it? I know. I've been there. This is the reason why I would share the ideas I've learned from my own experience of thesis writing.

What a thesis and why it is a must for every graduating college student to submit his/ her thesis? According to the definition, <u>thesis</u> pronounced as /THēsis/ is a statement or theory that is put forward as a premise to be maintained or proved. This is not something which is answerable by yes or no. This is something that you need to research, gather data, collate those data, analyze and synthesize them. Why are we required to do this? Most schools require that students complete a thesis or a project before graduating, though there are also schools who offer a non-thesis degree option, students enrolled in that program typically take more courses compare to those with thesis program. Besides, this is your chance to use the research and writing skills you learned in the program. This is your proof that you gained knowledge in your chosen field.

I assure you, thesis writing seems difficult when you see the long pattern, but, once you begin directing your effort and focus into it, you would eventually realize that it is not as difficult as you thought it was. What made me say that? I've been there. I had experienced the feeling of the doubt if I can do it or not. Trust me; the hardest thing is getting started. Just consider thesis writing as your summarized work and experience did in the program you're in and you have to complete the requirements (which includes thesis) to show your professors that you are ready for the culmination of your chosen degree. Yes, culmination. Isn't it exciting?

Finally, how I could make my own thesis? Well, that's a good question. Here are the simple guides:

It should be the topic that caught your interests and related to your chosen field so that you feel interested in doing your research and gathering of data. This would fuel your motivation to finish your thesis at all cost.

Begin with your thesis statement. The thesis statement should be clear and specific. Avoid vague words. As much as possible, avoid putting a thesis statement in the middle of a paragraph or late in the paper. Indicate the point of your paper but do it in a good way. Never use too obvious statement or a sentence like, "the point of my paper is this and that...." Originality is encouraged because of the point in your paper matters.

Finally, be diligent in gathering the data and record them accordingly so that it would be easier for you to analyze, synthesize and evaluate your work and arrive at a good, accurate conclusion.

Now that you already know the simple tips, I'll introduce you to the components of the thesis. Please note that I am not referring to dissertations since that is slightly different and much broader topic to discuss. Are you ready to take a leap?

PART II. COMPONENTS OF A THESIS

Preliminaries:

Cover page/title page- it displays thesis title, candidate's name, qualifications, thesis details, department, university and date

Table of Contents- it has the lists of all major divisions and chapter titles

List of tables/figures/illustrations

Summary/Abstract-this summarizes the research undertaken in order to provide an overview of the project and its significance.

Acknowledgments-this recognize the help given by the people who offered support or advice.

TEXT OF THE THESIS

Introduction- provides a clear statement of the topic/problem under investigation and provides the general context for the research sometimes giving details of the methodology and the theoretical background and usually outlining applications of the research. It forcefully justifies the need for this research and states the aims.

Literature Review- presents a critical review of relevant previous studies in the research field. This chapter shows how knowledge has been built up in the research field and, by clearly demonstrating the achievements but also the limitations of the previous research, it presents a well-argued justification for the research to be undertaken.

Sequential Chapters present a detailed description of the experimental or theoretical work undertaken, the results and a discussion of the significance of these results. Each chapter usually has a brief introduction which states the aim of the chapter and an outline of its structure, as well as a short summary to highlight the significant findings of the chapter.

Conclusions and recommendations- presents the major conclusions which can be drawn from the findings of the research. This chapter also makes recommendations for further research.

References/Bibliography- records all works that have been referred to in the text of the thesis.

Of course, I won't leave you hanging with those ideas. I will share a sample research paper in the following chapter.

PART III. SAMPLE RESEARCH PAPER

The following thesis is a sample one. That is our work as a requirement to pass the research subject, (me and my classmate, Ms. Sarah Balagso). We're sharing it to you with the hope you would find it useful. Enjoy reading.

Republic of the Philippines
POLYTECHNIC UNIVERSITY OF THE PHILIPPINES
Santa Rosa City, Laguna

October 23, 2016

Concept Paper for:

WORK – LIFE BALANCE: A LOOK AT TEACHERS' SPILLOVER
EFFECTS

In Partial Fulfillment of the Requirements for the Degree of Master of
Arts in Educational Management

Submitted by: MEM STUDENTS

Ms. FREALYN M. NAVARRO

Ms. SARAH C. BALAGSO

Submitted to:

DR. ROSALIE A. CORPUS

CHAPTER 1

THE PROBLEM AND ITS BACKGROUND

Introduction

Work life balance among teachers is one of the most subject research nowadays. It has been found in some research that teaching is a stressful profession (Rosser, 2004). Clark (1989) concluded that it is the teaching profession that has different dimensions such as a pattern of work, authority, identification and career and so on. Winslow and Jacobs (2004) find out the relationship between faculty workload and their dissatisfaction.

It is a common challenge to teachers how to weigh personal life concerns and work-life concerns and these challenges will directly affect teacher's performance at work or at home.

Time matters. The distance from home to school could be a factor, too. In some rural areas in the Philippines like in Mindanao, some teachers need to travel far in a risky ride to fulfill their duty. The daily transportation stress would impact teacher's health and would lead to either tardiness or late. Luckily in Santa Rosa Science and Technology High School, most teachers live near the school campus thus, time travel will only take a few minutes from home to school.

Teachers are also a husband/wife at home and they also have responsibilities to do. These responsibilities sometimes affect the teacher's attitude towards work. If she/he is already exhausted at home and no time to have at least recreation because of home to work routine, both will be affected; thus life and work balance may hard to meet due to these circumstances.

In reality, benefits like adequacy of salaries and wages is good news. No matter how high is the expectation and workload, as long as the compensation is great, this would help teachers to keep going and be motivated simply because they don't need to worry about financial matters as their work already provided it to them. The thought of having financial security is quite enough to make every end meet and less worry on the part of the teachers.

In Santa Rosa Science and Technology High School, the community and teachers help each other in terms of students' welfare and development. Parents are also cooperative and teachers have harmonious and open communication with one another.

Background of the Study

Santa Rosa Science and Technology High School has a total number of 48 teaching and non-teaching staff and one principal. The school is located in the heart of Santa Rosa City, Laguna near the public market, community hospital and local government office. The community where the school is located is safe and accessible to important landmarks. We just started the senior high school programs offering Science,

Technology, Engineering, and Mathematics to prepare the students as they pursue higher education programs related to their interests and skills.

Teachers, parents, and community, as I observe, work together for a common good. We have open communication and most of the teachers are also from the same locality. Parents send feedback and the school address the feedback timely to avoid misunderstanding between educators and parents.

Theoretical Framework

The most popular view of the relationship between work and family was put forth by Piotkowski in his Spillover Theory (1979). He suggested that workers carry the emotions, attitudes, skills, and behaviors that they establish at work into their family life. Spillover can be positive or negative. Positive spillover refers to the fact that satisfaction and achievement in one domain may bring along satisfaction and achievement in another domain. Negative spillover refers to the fact that difficulties and depression in one domain may bring along the same emotion in another domain. (Xu, 2009)

The Spillover Crossover Model supports the theory stated above. According to Bakker et al., 2008 – 2009, Spillover Crossover Model was recently formulated stating that strain built up at work (including perceptions of inequity) may spill over to the home domain by having an impact on (reduced) helping or (increased) undermining behaviors.

Researchers have identified two different ways in which demands or strain is carried over: spillover and crossover. Negative Spillover or work-family conflict is a within-person across-domains transmission of demands and consequent strain from one area of life to another. Work-family conflict is defined as "a form of inter-role conflict in which the role pressures from the work and family domains are mutually incompatible in some respect. That is, participation in the work (family) role is made more difficult by virtue of participation in the family (work) role."

In contrast to spillover, crossover involves transmission across individuals, whereby demands and their consequent strain cross over between closely related persons (Westman, 2002). Thus, in a crossover, stress experienced in the workplace by an individual may lead to stress being experienced by the individual's partner at home. Whereas spillover is an intra-individual transmission of stress or strain, a crossover is a dyadic, inter-individual transmission of stress or strain.

Clark (2000) presented a work/family border theory – a new theory about family balance. According to this theory, each of a person's role takes place within a specific domain of life, and these domains are separated that may be physical, temporal or psychological. The theory addresses the issue of "crossing border" between domains of life, especially the domain of home and work.

According to the theory, the flexibility and permeability of the boundaries between people's work and family lives will affect the level of integration, the ease of transitions, and the level of conflict between these domains Boundaries that are flexible and permeable facilitate integration between work and home domains. When domains are relatively integrated, the transition is easier, but the work-family conflict is more likely. Conversely, when these domains are segmented, the transition is more effortful, but the work-family conflict is less likely. (Bellavia and Frone, 2005)

These theories attempt to generate a model that would describe the state of work and family life balance. These help to examine the work and family balance of the respondents to be used as bases for formulating sound recommendations that would specifically address the right to maintain a healthy family life as they commit themselves to the goals of education.

Conceptual Framework

The conceptual framework demonstrated is organized information. This study was made to find the spillover effect on the job performance of the study's respondents

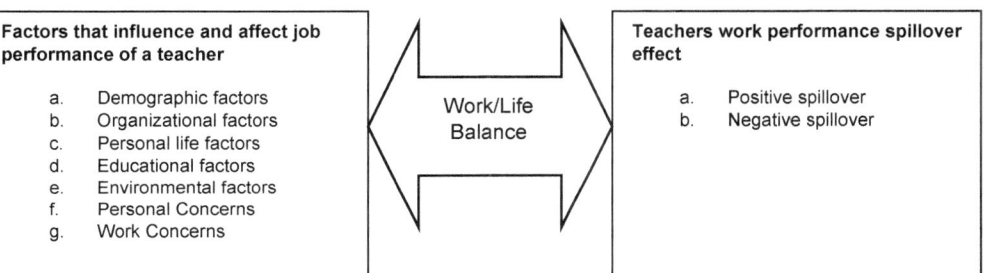

Figure 1: Conceptual Framework

This figure conceptualizes the spillover effect of the work/life balance on the job performance of teachers. The first box contains the factors that influence the job performance of the respondents (Demographic, Organizational, Personal, Educational, Environmental, Personal and Work Concerns) that will guide to show the result on the work/life balance of teachers.

The second box shows the spillover effects on the job performances of teachers which may be positive or negative.

The arrow indicates the relationship between these two variables.

Statement of the Problem

This study aims to examine the Spillover effects of work-life balance on the job performance of teachers in the Santa Rosa Science and Technology High School.

Specifically, this study sought to answer the following sub-problems:

1. What is the respondents' personal data in terms of:

    1.1   Age

    1.2   Sex

    1.3   Civil Status

    1.4   Highest educational attainment

    1.5   Current designation at school

    1.6   No. of hours travel from home to school

    1.7   Public or Private school

    1.8   No. of students handled

    1.9   Employment status

    1.10   Length of service as a teacher

    1.11   Level handled?

2. What are the respondents' perceptions of the factors that influence the job performance of a teacher, in terms of:

    2.1   Demographic factors;

    2.2   Organizational factors;

    2.3   Personal life factors;

2.4   Educational factors; and

2.5   Environmental factors?

3. What are the respondents' perceptions of concerns that may affect his/her performance on the job as a teacher in terms of:

3.1 Personal life concerns; and

3.2 Work life concerns?

4. Is there a significant relationship between the factors that influence the job performance of a teacher and the spillover effects of their work performance?

5. Is there a significant relationship between the respondents' concerns that may affect his/her performance on the job and the spillover effects of their work performance?

Hypotheses

There are two null hypotheses that will be tested at 0.5% degree of significance:

1. There is a significant relationship between the factors that influence the job performance of a teacher and the spillover effects of their work performance.

2. There is a significant relationship between the respondents' concerns that may affect his/her performance on the job and the spillover effects of their work performance?

Scope and Limitations of the Study

The research study focused on determining the spillover effects of the teachers' work/life balance as they practice their profession as educators This study is limited to Santa Rosa Science and Technology High School which has a total of 32 teaching force. 25 of the respondents are from Junior high school and only 7 respondents from Senior high school.

Data collected were compared using an appropriate statistical tool. A total of 32 teachers were considered as samples which are then generalized as the sources of data collected. The respondents were provided with questionnaires to answer pertaining to their demographic profile and their perceptions on work-life balance spillover among teachers.

Significance of the Study

This study is anticipated to contribute additional information to serve the following individuals.

School Administrator. This study served as a tool that greatly influences the school administrators' decision in planning teacher education programs and courses.

Teachers. This study served as teachers' guide to determine those possible causes of spillover and eventually provide and promote the proper balance of life at home and at work. Lessen the burden and look for further ways to self-motivate and move forward.

Definition of Terms

For better understanding and interpretation of this study, the following terms are operationally and theoretically defined.

Spillover- [spill·o·ver]

*As used in this study, this refers to a secondary effect that follows the primary effect and may be far removed in time or placed from the event that causes the primary effect. It has positive and negative spillover. For example, Odors from a rendering plant are negative spillover effects upon its neighbors; the beauty of a homeowner's flower garden is a positive spillover effect upon neighbors.)

Job Performance

*Relates to the act of doing a job. Job performance is a means to reach a goal or set of goals within a job, role, or organization but not the actual consequences of the acts performed within a job. It is not a single action but rather a "complex activity". Performance in a job is strictly a behavior and a separate entity from the outcomes of a particular job which relate to success and productivity.

Demographic factors

*Personal characteristics are used to collect and evaluate data on people in a given population. Typical factors include age, gender, marital status, race, education, income, and occupation.

Organizational structure

*It is the framework companies use to outline their authority and communication processes. The framework usually includes policies, rules, and responsibilities for each individual in the organization. Several factors affect the organizational structure of a company. These factors can be internal or external.

Educational equity

*Referred to as equity in education, is a measure of achievement, fairness, and opportunity in education. The second important factor is inclusion, which refers to a comprehensive standard that applies to everyone in a certain education system.

Environmental Factor

*An identifiable element in the physical, cultural, demographic, economic, political, regulatory, or technological environment that affects the survival, operations, and growth of an organization.

Personal life

*It is the course of an individual's life, especially when viewed as the sum of personal. Other factors affecting personal life are individuals' health, personal relationships, pets as well as home and personal possessions.

Work–life balance

*It is a concept including proper prioritizing between "work" (career and ambition) and "lifestyle" (health, pleasure, leisure, family and spiritual development/meditation). This is related to the idea of lifestyle choice.

CHAPTER 2

REVIEW OF RELATED LITERATURE AND STUDIES

This chapter presents a review of the literature which had a direct bearing on the present study. It also presents some other findings of other researchers which can add support in administration of the study

The spillover has positive and negative effects. Poor unwinding concerns the disability to relax and disconnect from work. It represents spillover between life domains (Grebner, Semmer & Elfering, 2005; Mohr, Rigotti & Muller, 2005).

Results of this study reveal that although work-related stress and home-related stress are both significantly correlated with work-family conflict, it is work-related stress that predicts work-family conflict.The findings validate the results in a previous study that Filipino working parents report work as the predominant source of stress (Hechanova, 2005). More stress to deal with at work implies less time with family that very likely explains the experienced work-family conflict. In Hechanova's (2005) study, working parents identified spending moretime with family as their primary concern. The study also reveals that some working mothers, in particular, appear to have a sense of guilt. As one mother in her study recounted, "more than anything that is difficult to shake is the ever-present feeling of guilt that I'm not being a good mom because I have a career" (p. 32).

With respect to antecedents, domain specific antecedents are the best predictors for both works to family conflicts and family-to-work conflicts. Domain specific predictors mean in this context that works demands, such as time pressure or conflicts with supervisors, are domain specific predictors for work to family demands, such as high responsibility for one's children in a dangerous situation or conflicts with one's spouse are domain specific predictors for family-to-work conflicts. See Eby, Caspar, Lockwood, Bordeaux & Brinley, 2005; Byron, 2005 for reference.

A study by Aguirre-Mateo (2005) showed a positive relationship between Filipino employees' satisfaction with their company's work-life initiatives and life satisfaction.Thus, family-friendly benefits and programs maybe an important means to empower especially dual-career couples to juggle their roles. Organizations can also provide stress and time management workshops to help their employees better manage and balance their work and family life. The study highlights the role of personal social support. Interestingly, it is the personal social support that moderates the relationship between home-related stress and marital satisfaction. Perhaps personal support frees up time for working parents to not just focus on their role as workers and parents but also on strengthening their bond as a couple. Or at the very least, adequate support may mean less conflict among working parents.

Kiger et al, 2007 found that high levels of satisfaction with how housework was delegated decreased negative home-to-work spillover. These results suggest the importance of considering perceptions of home and family life, not just time constraint factors at home when attempting to identify predictors of negative spillover from home to work.

As more and more women enter the workforce, the issue of work-family conflict will become more important. Juggling workand family isdifficult and it becomes even more challenging when both spouses are doing this.Yet the reality is that dual incomes are becoming a necessity given our difficult times. The challenge then is how employers, families and other social networks support working parents. Hilary Clinton (1996) once said that it takes a village to raise a child. In the modem world, it appears that is certainly true. (Ortega & Hechanova, 2010)

In relation to occupational characteristics, educational characteristics may also be important factors associated with negative spillover. A higher level of education to be associated with a higher level of negative home-to-work spillover (Brayfield et al.; Voydanoff, 2005). Individuals with higher levels occupy employment positions that are more demanding or require longer hours of work. These results would be consistent that found individuals employed as professionals and individuals feeling time pressure on the job were more likely to experience negative home-to-work spillover.

Synthesis

All the given reviewed literature and studies served as guide references to the present study. The materials helped the researcher in her effort to clarify the problem investigated and the methods used in this study.

In terms of similarity, it is more likely of Aguirre-Mateo (2005) wherein family-friendly benefits and programs may be an important means to empower especially dual-career couples to juggle their roles. However, at some point, this study is slightly different because most of the respondents have high willingness to fulfill their duties while trying to balance with their personal life. Most of the respondents are female and most of them are 6-10 years in service.

While it is true that Individuals with higher levels occupy employment positions that are more demanding or require longer hours of work according to (Brayfield et al.; Voydanoff, 2005), however in this study, most of the respondents are satisfied with their work and if we base on the length of their service, it is remarkably good.

CHAPTER 3

METHODOLOGY

This chapter presents the research design used, the respondents of the study, instrumentation, data gathering procedures, and the statistical treatment of data.

Research Design

This research project utilized the descriptive method of research. Descriptive research is the description and characteristics of an existing phenomenon, a problem, issue or certain situation, designed to provide systematic information regarding them. It is a research process by which the data gathered was organized and analyzed. Thereafter, significant conclusions were derived. The focus of the whole process is the discovery of meaning through comparison of finding relationships of one kind or another. The process goes beyond near gathering and tabulating of data. It involves interpretation of the meaning of significance of "what is" described (Sanchez 2002). This study also made use of quantitative method of research which focuses heavily on standardized and numerical data as well as statistical analysis when it comes to the process of collecting data, the nature of the instrument in data collection and the kind of strategy to be employed in order to analyse the data (Johnson and Christensen, 2004). This approach was deemed to provide teachers the opportunity to rate the percentage and frequency of the spillover effect of the work/life balance of teachers as they practice their profession as educators.

Respondents of the Study

The subject respondents of this study are teachers of Santa Rosa Science and Technology High School in the Division of Santa Rosa City. The composition of the subject respondents is 25 junior high school teachers and 7 senior high school teachers to determine their perception of the factors that influence the job performance of a teacher as well as their perception of work and personal concerns that may affect their performance on the job. Their responses will also be used to assess their level of agreement with implications of the spillover effects of their job as teachers.

Table 1

Respondents of the Study

Category of Respondents	Frequency	Percentage
Junior High School Teachers	25	78.125%
Senior High School Teachers	7	21.875%
Total	32	100%

Table 1 shows that majority of the respondents came from a junior high school with a percentage of 78.125%. Only 21.875% are respondents from senior high school.

Table 2

Profile of the Respondents in Terms of Age

Age	Frequency	Percentage
21 – 25	2	6.250%
26 – 30	6	18.750%
31 – 35	9	28.125%
36 – 40	5	15.625%
41 – 45	4	12.500%
46 – 50	2	6.250%
51 – 55	3	9.375%
56 and above	1	3.125%
Total	32	100%

Table 2 shows the percentage distribution of the respondents' age. Age bracket 31 – 35 years old has the highest frequency with a corresponding percentage of 28.125%. Six (6) or 18.750% are 26 – 30 years old, followed by five (5) respondents for 36 – 40 years old or 15.625%, four (4) for 41 – 45 years old or 12.500%, three (3) for 51 – 55 years old or 9.375%, both two (2) or 6.250% for 46 – 50 and 21 -25 years old and only one (1) respondent for the age bracket 56 years old and above.

Table 3

Profile of Respondents in Terms of Gender

Gender	Frequency	Percentage
Male	9	28.125%
Female	23	71.875%
Total	32	100%

Table 3 shows the gender of the respondents. There are twenty-three (23) or 71.875% female and nine (9) or 28.125% male. It was observed that majority of the respondents of this study are female teachers.

Table 4

Profile of Respondents in Terms of Civil Status

Civil Status	Frequency	Percentage
Single	11	34.375%
Married	19	59.375%
Widowed	2	6.250%
Separated	0	0%
Total	32	100%

Table 4 shows the percentage distribution of the respondents' civil status. It was revealed that most of the respondents are married with a frequency of nineteen (19) or 59.375%; followed by eleven (11) single status respondents. Two (2) out of 32 respondents or 6.250% are widowed and no one is separated.

Table 5

Profile of Respondents in Terms of Highest Educational Attainment

Highest Educational Attainment	Frequency	Percentage
Bachelor's Degree	11	34.375%
With M.A. units	13	40.625%
Master's Degree	7	21.875%
With Doctorate units	1	3.125%
Doctorate Degree	0	0%
Total	32	100%

Table 5 shows the percentage distribution of the respondents' highest educational attainment. Thirteen (13) or 40.625% earned units in Master's degree, eleven (11) or 34.375% finishedBachelor's degree, seven (7) or 21.875% are Master's degree holders, and only one (1) or 3.125% acquired Doctorate units. No one is Doctorate degree holder.

Table 6

Profile of Respondents in Terms of Current Designation at School

Designation	Frequency	Percentage
Teacher I	18	56.250%
Teacher II	4	12.500%
Teacher III	5	15.625%
Head Teacher I	2	6.250%
Master Teacher I	1	3.125%
Master Teacher II	2	6.250%
Total	32	100%

Table 6 shows the percentage distribution of the respondents' current designation at school. It was depicted that majority of the respondents are Teacher I (56.250%), followed by Teacher III (15.625%), Teacher II (12.500%), Head Teacher I and Master Teacher II obtained the same frequency of 2 (6.250%), and Master Teacher I had the least frequency (3.125%).

Table 7

Profile of Respondents in Terms of the No. of Hours Travel from Home to School

Travel Time	Frequency	Percentage
1 – 10 min.	7	21.875%
11 – 20 min.	11	34.375%
21 – 30 min.	5	15.625%
31 – 40 min.	0	0%
41 – 50 min.	1	3.125%
51 – 60 min.	7	21.875%
More than 60 min.	1	3.125%
Total	32	100%

Table 7 shows the percentage distribution of the respondents' number of hours travels from home to school. It was revealed that most of the respondent's travel time is 11 – 20 min. with a percentage of 34.375%. Both 1 – 10 min. and 51 – 60 min. travel time obtained the same percentage of 21.875%. Followed by 21 – 30 min. travel time with a percentage of 15.625%; the same percentage of 3.125% was obtained for travel time41 – 50 min. and More than 60 min. No one travels 31 – 40 min. from home to school.

Table 8

Profile of Respondents in Terms of School Category

School Category	Frequency	Percentage
Public	32	100%
Private	0	0%
Total	32	100%

Table 8 shows the percentage distribution of the respondents' school category. All (100%) of the respondents are in public school.

Table 9

Profile of Respondents in Terms of No. of Students Handled

No. of Students Handled	Frequency	Percentage
0 – 49	1	3.125%
50 – 99	1	3.125%
100 – 149	0	0%
150 – 199	8	25.000%
200 – 249	10	31.250%
250 – 299	10	31.250%
300and Above	2	6.250%
Total	32	100%

Table 9 shows the percentage distribution of the respondents' number of students handled. The majority of the respondents handled 200 – 249 and 250 – 299 students with a percentage of 31.250%. Eight or 25.000% of the respondents handled 150 – 199 students. Two (2) or 6.250% handled 300 students and above. One (1) respondent or 3.125% handled both 0 – 49 and 50 – 99 students. No one handled 100 – 149 students.

Table 10

Profile of Respondents in Terms of Employment Status

Employment Status	Frequency	Percentage
Probationary	0	0%
Regular Permanent	32	100%
Total	32	100%

Table 10 shows the percentage distribution of the respondents' employment status. All (100%) respondents have employment status of regular permanent.

Table 11

Profile of Respondents in Terms of Length of Service as a Teacher

No. of Years in Service as a Teacher	Frequency	Percentage
1 – 5 years	5	15.625%
6 – 10 years	11	34.375%
11 – 15 years	9	28.125%
16 – 20 years	4	12.500%
More than 20 years	3	9.375%
Total	32	100%

Table 11 shows the percentage distribution of the respondents' length of service as a teacher. Most of the respondents have been in the service for 6 – 10 years with a percentage of 34.375%, nine (9) or 28.125% for 11 – 15 years, five (5) or 15.625% for 1 – 5 years, four (4) or 12.500% for 16 – 20 years, and only three (3) or 9.375% rendered service as a teacher for more than 20 years.

Table 12

Profile of Respondents in Terms of Grade Level Handled

Grade Level	Frequency	Percentage
Grade 7	4	12.500%
Grade 8	4	12.500%
Grade 9	5	15.625%
Grade 10	7	21.875%
Grade 11	7	21.875%
More than one grade level	5	15.625%
Total	32	100%

Table 12 shows the percentage distribution of the respondents' grade level handling. The majority of the respondents handled grade 10 and 11 garnering 21.875%; 15.625% handled grade 9 and more than one grade level. The least number of respondents handled grade 7 and 8 with both percentages of 12.500%.

Instrumentation

The main data-gathering instrument of the study is the questionnaire provided by the adviser.

The first part of the survey questionnaire intends to elicit information on the profile of the respondents.

The second part aimed to determine the respondent's perception of the factors that influence the job performance of as a teacher.

The third part is the respondent's perception of work and personal concerns that may affect his/her performance on the job.

The last part is the respondent's level of agreement with implications of the spillover effects of their job as teacher.

Data Gathering Procedures

The questionnaire was personally administered to the teachers as respondents of the study. The following data gathering procedure was initiated: a.) administration of the survey questionnaires, b.) proper supervision with instructions for the respondents to properly answer the given questions, c.) collection of the answered survey-questionnaires, d.) recording on the tally sheet the different levels of answers by the respondents, and e.) after consolidation and tabulation, the researchers discussed, analyzed, and interpreted the results in accordance with the statement of the problem.

Statistical Treatment of Data

The following were the statistical tools applied in the study:

1. To determine the respondents' perception of the factors that influence the job performance of a teacher as well as their perception of work and personal concerns that may affect their performance on the job the four-point Modified Scale and the simple mean were used. The formula for the mean is given as

$$\bar{x} = \frac{\sum_{i=1}^{n} x_i}{N}$$

where $\bar{x}$ is the simple mean, $\sum_{i=1}^{n} x_i$ is the sum of all values of variable x, and N is the number of respondents. Furthermore, interpretations for computed means were adopted from the following:

On the Perception of the Factors that Influence the Job Performance of a Teacher

Arbitrary Scale	Interpretation
3.50 – 4.00	With High Influence
2.50 – 3.49	With Influence
1.50 – 2.49	With Some Influence
1.00 – 1.49	With No Influence

On the Level of Agreement with Implications of the Spillover Effects of the Respondent's as Teacher

Arbitrary Scale	Interpretation
3.50 – 4.00	Strongly Agree
2.50 – 3.49	Agree
1.50 – 2.49	Moderately Agree
1.00 – 1.49	Do Not Agree

2. The frequency and percent distributions were used in presenting the routine personal and work life concerns of a teacher that may affect his/her performance on the job. The percent formula is

$$\% = \frac{frequency}{total\ population} x\ 100\%$$

3. To determine the relationship between the factors that influence the job performance of a teacher and the spillover effects of their work performance, the Pearson correlation coefficient was used. The same statistical tool was used to find out the relationship between the respondents' concerns that may affect their performance on the job and the spillover effects of their work performance. The formula is given as:

$$r = \frac{n\sum xy - \sum x \cdot \sum y}{\sqrt{\left[n\sum x^2 - \left(\sum x\right)^2\right]\left[n\sum y^2 - \left(\sum y\right)^2\right]}}$$

*To interpret the computed Pearson correlation coefficient, the following guide was adopted:

coefficient	Interpretation
± 1.00	Perfect Positive/Negative Correlation
± 0.76 - ±0.99	Very High Positive/Negative Correlation
± 0.51 - ±0.75	High Positive/Negative Correlation
± 0.26 - ±0.50	Small Positive/Negative Correlation
± 0.01 - ±0.25	Very Small Positive/Negative Correlation
00 00	No Correlation

CHAPTER 4

PRESENTATION AND ANALYSIS OF FINDINGS

This chapter presents the pertinent data gathered, the analysis done as well as its corresponding interpretations. The discussion is divided into three parts. The first part tackles the perceptions of the respondents in the factors that influence the job performance of a teacher. The middle part involves the respondents' perceptions on personal and work life concerns of a teacher that may affect their performance on the job. The last part discusses the respondents' level of agreement with implications of the spillover effects of their job as a teacher.

The majority of the respondents came from the junior high school with a percentage of 78.125%. Only 21.875% are respondents from senior high school.

Most of the respondents' age bracket ranging from 31 – 35 years old have the highest frequency with a corresponding percentage of 28.125%. Six (6) or 18.750% are 26 – 30 years old, followed by five (5) respondents for 36 – 40 years old or 15.625%, four (4) for 41 – 45 years old or 12.500%, three (3) for 51 – 55 years old or 9.375%, both two (2) or 6.250% for 46 – 50 and 21 -25 years old and only one (1) respondent for the age bracket 56 years old and above.

The majority of the respondents are female garnering (23) or 71.875%, and only nine (9) or 28.125% are males. It was observed that majority of the respondents of this study are female teachers. Most of the respondents are married with a total of 59.375% or equivalent to (19) respondents; while 11 respondents are single; and only 2 of the respondents are the widow.

In terms of highest educational attainment, the study reveals that no one holds a doctorate degree. One respondent has acquired doctorate units while 7 of them are master's degree holder; 11 respondents have bachelor's degree and 13 of them earns masters degree units. The majority of respondents are Teacher I (56.250%); followed by Teacher III (15.625%); Teacher II (12.500%) same as Head Teacher I and Master Teacher II while Master Teacher I has the least frequency of 3.125%.

With respect to travel time, study shows that most of the respondents travel time is 11 – 20 min with a garnering 34.375% of the respondents both male and female; while 21.875% of the respondents travel 1 – 10 min. and the same percentage of those respondents who travel 51 – 60 min. Only 15.625% of the respondents consume 21 – 30 min. travel time; while 3.125% of the respondents travel time is 41 – 50 min. but not more than 60 min. No one travels 31 – 40 min. from home to school.

All of the respondents are from public school.In terms of the number of students handled, the majority of the respondents handled 200 – 249 and 250 – 299 students with a percentage of 31.250%. Eight or 25.000% of the respondents handled 150 – 199 students. Two (2) or 6.250% handled 300 students and above. One (1) respondent or 3.125% handled both 0 – 49 and 50 – 99 students. No one handled 100 – 149 students.

All (100%) respondents have employment status of regular permanent. Most of the respondents have been in the service for 6 – 10 years with a total percentage of 34.375%, nine (9) or 28.125% for 11 – 15 years, five (5) or 15.625% for 1 – 5 years, four (4) or 12.500% for 16 – 20 years, and only three (3) or 9.375% rendered service as a teacher for more than 20 years.

The majority of the respondents handled grade 10 and 11 garnering 21.875%; 15.625% handled grade 9 and more than one grade level. The least number of respondents handled grade 7 and 8 with only 12.500%.

Based on the data gathered, since the majority of the respondents stayed in the school serves more than six to ten years while some rendered for more than 20 years, it is remarkable to note that the respondents are happy and satisfied. Therefore, they experience positive spillover from their respective position. Based on fact that there are numbers of respondents who are having units of master's degree while some are master's degree holder, it is quite evident that they are empowering themselves for a possible higher position with respect to the degrees they earned. Well aware that having higher position means higher responsibility on their part.

CHAPTER 5

CONCLUSIONS AND RECOMMENDATIONS

This chapter presents the findings, the corresponding conclusions derived from these findings as well as the recommendations based on the findings and conclusions.

Based on the data gathered, researchers conclude that Santa Rosa Science and Technology High School experience a positive spillover in terms of their respective position and task handled.

Despite the changing needs of the teaching field, teachers cope up and empower themselves through acquiring higher degrees of education to fulfill their duties and responsibilities inside and outside of school.

As part of the recommendation, it would be best to look forward to the majority of teachers with either master's degree holder or doctorate degree holder, respectively to gauge more of their satisfaction in their job as an educator and the best of their students and family welfare.

Life and work balance is attainable and doable, too. It needs to be properly aligned and manage to make sure that despite the workload; teachers can still balance their time with their family. In the end, it is the maturity of character that will define us as teachers as we mold the next generation of professionals where we are best known of.

Bibliography

Abustan, Kino (2010). **Modalities in Teaching Mathematics in the Intermediate Level in the Division of Laguna.**

Barbara (2012) GMA News online. www.gma.com

Benito (2009). Analysis of the Performance in Trigonometry of the First Year College Students of Divine World College of Vigan.www. scribd .com

Biancarosa, Bryk A. S., and Dexter E. R, (2010). Assessing the Value-Added Effects of Literacy Collaborative Professional Development of Student Learning.

Campbell, Patricia F. et.al. (2014). The Relationship Between Teachers' Mathematical Content and Pedagogical Knowledge, Teachers' Perceptions, and Student Achievement.

Claveria, Janette O. (2014). Strategies in Teaching Intermediate Mathematics and Problem Solving Skills Development in Selected Public Schools in Cabuyao, Laguna.

Corpuz, et.al.(2013). Principles of Teaching, Lorimar Publishing Inc. 3rd Edition.

Muthaa, George M. et.al.(2012). Factors Contributing to Students' Poor Performance in Mathematics at Kenya.American International Journal of Contemporary Research.National Council of Teachers and Mathematics, Principles, and Standards for School Mathematics 2000.

Parada, Paulo E. (2013). Factors Affecting the Achievement of High School Students in Mathematics at San Juan National High School.

Saritas, Tuncancy, and Akademir, Omur (2009). Identifying Factors Affecting the Mathematics Achievement of Students for Better Instructional Design.

Suan, Joefel S. (2014). Factors Affecting Underachievement in Mathematics.

Subramanian, Kennedy (2010). Drawing From Cognitive Studies of Mathematical Learning for Curriculum Design.

Triphati, Pretty N. (2009). Problem Solving in Mathematics: A Tool for Cognitive Development. University of the Philippines.

Wei, et. al. (2009). Professional Development in the United States: Trends and Challenges.

Workman, Teri A. (2012). Students Attitudes on Learning.

Zulueta, Francisco M. (2009). Principles and Methods of Teaching.

PART IV. GENERALIZATION

We have finally shared the ideas that we truly desire to spread out so that those self-doubts would be replaced with the feeling of "I can do it, too!" claim. No need to complicate things. We desire that by now, you realized that thesis writing could be fun to do as well. This is the reflection of what you have learned, better be proud you learned.   I appreciate your time reading this book and I would love to hear your feedback and comment in Amazon site

www.ingramcontent.com/pod-product-compliance
Lightning Source LLC
Chambersburg PA
CBHW050833290526
45792CB00001B/381